TOGETHER WE CAN SAVE THE HIGH STREET

A book of unique ideas that have the potential to save the high street

IAN MASON

Ian Mason

Save The High Street

Ian Mason

Save The High Street

CONTENTS

Ian Mason

Save The High Street

INTRODUCTION (1)

In this book, we'll be going through ideas on how we can save the high street; but not in the traditional sense. We will be exploring a unique way to save the high street. Not by solely blaming online shopping, but instead reinventing what a high street stands for. We need to make the high street more than just a place to buy things, we need to advertise an experience and connect the high street with people on an emotional level. We will explore what this means in more detail in the following chapters.

A quote from Steve Jobs: "Marketing is about values". He needed Apple to represent values, that people will always remember them by. Because we live in a very complicated and noisy world and in order for Apple to survive, Apple needed something to put them out there. In this book we will take this concept, and apply it on a much larger scale.

There's room for both online shopping and high street shopping. But we need to make the high street something more, than just 'shops'. We need to turn it into something that makes people want to leave their home and go out to shop.

WHY SAVE THE HIGH STREET? (2)

The high street is more than just a place to go and shop. It has the potential to bring people and communities together. People going shopping with their friends. People establishing new connections, whether it's through jobs or just happen to 'click' with your fellow shoppers.

If you go shopping at your local high street, you may notice that no one communicates with their fellow shoppers, they just browse on their own in silence or are hanging out with people that they already know. However, it doesn't have to be like this, you see; the high street can be a cure for loneliness. We should be encouraging communication with other shoppers. I'll give you an example: a man walks in looking for a nice shirt, he goes up to someone and asks 'do you think this looks good on me?' The person who is at the receiving end can then answer accordingly and a conversation can carry on from there. People are to afraid to speak to random people, there's a 'fear' that people have when speaking to strangers and it's understandable why. People don't respect each other as much as they used to, people are worried that the other person may be a bad individual. But this is the thinking process that has caused our communities to be weakened. It's only a small minority that are bad individuals. The vast majority of people are just like you and me, and are more than happy to have a conversation with you. We just need to normalise it, and the best way to normalise things, is through televised ads and celebrities getting involved. We can change the general culture. We can make it cool to speak to strangers. There's a risk to everything in life, you can go for a drive and there's a chance you can end up in a car accident. But we can't ban driving because of it. Encouraging communication with fellow shoppers should be a must; this can not only save the high street, it can also create new friendships. There's plenty of people out there who are lonely and have no one to talk to and could use a healthy conversation with people.

When you go to a busy high street, what do you see? You see street performers showing off their talents to the community and the world. You see people gathering round; admiring their talents and recording them. Street performers have a tremendous amount of confidence to go up there and perform in front of everyone, it's admirable and inspiring to witness. They gain attention from performing in front of the public. You can say that they can perform on the internet, but you don't know how long that will take to reach people. It takes a while to gain attention on the web. But you can instantly gain attention when you just go out there and perform in front of people while they all have their phones out and showing it off on their social media stories. You can say that they can perform at the train stations, but generally everyone is in a rush to get to work or wherever they need to be, they don't want to be standing round watching a performance. The high street is the best opportunity to do these things. If the high street dies, street performers get stripped of opportunity.

What else does the high street offer? Well the most obvious one is jobs! Lots of them! They may not be 'high paying'. But so many people love their jobs on the high street, many people don't think so, they think everyone who works in jobs like these hate their jobs. This simply isn't the case, there's many people who establish new friendships when working in these stores, it's a place for them to hang out, earn money and save the money, so they can potentially go travelling in the future, or whatever their dream is.

The high street is also a great starting point to receive experience and to enter into the working environment. Some people establish a career on working within the high street, they can work their way up from the bottom and possibly reach a management position, or the people who get the management job from the get-go, also have their livelihoods to protect, and if the high street dies, it will be absolutely devastating to so many people and families out there. Not everyone wants to advance themselves into a different field of work, they want to do a job that they enjoy, and if they enjoy their job on the high street, then that shouldn't be taken away from them. Forcing people into a career path they don't want to take can be extremely stressful and depressing for those individuals. Not everyone works for the money, some people work because they enjoy it and it gives them a sense of purpose in life. Jobs like these can also help those who have problems socialising with people, when they are involved in customer service; communication with the customers can really boost their confidence and get them to develop communication skills. It's jobs like these, that can help people who struggle with addiction, it can take it off their minds for the day. It's jobs like these that are a vital part of our communities.

These jobs are the backbone of many working class and even middle class families out there. Imagine if you were a husband or a wife, with kids; you may have a good job, but it's still not enough to pay off debts and support your family. So you ask your son or your daughter, to get a part time job while they're at school. There's not many options out there for them, they don't have qualifications or any experience. What job would accept them? Well, working on the high street, can be a source of extra income for the family and helps your son or daughter gain experience in the working environment.

Save The High Street

The people who do shop on the high street, generally do so because they like to touch & feel the product, they like to try things on before a purchase. It's people like this, who would much rather talk to a person behind the counter, than through a computer. Many people don't mind either way, which is why those people need motivation to leave the house and visit the high street. If some consumers don't like shopping online, they are less likely to spend their money doing so, the high street needs to be saved so that these people are more willing to spend their money and to contribute more to the economy as a whole.

The high street gives towns and villages some life, it makes it vibrant. Nobody wants to live in a dead town with nothing in it; it'll make these places unwelcoming and you're not encouraging people to move and buy a home in the country if most towns are in a derelict state.

There's so many reasons why the high street is worth saving, of which some; I'm probably not aware of. You have probably got your own reasons as to why you think the high street should be saved. Which is why we must save it, because it's a vital element of our society.

Ian Mason

HOW CAN WE SAVE THE HIGH STREET? (3)

Saving the high street requires both small and large businesses that operate on the high street, to form together an organisation, of which, they can all contribute the funds needed to save it. The organisation needs to establish a name for itself, let's just call it 'operation save the high street' for this example. This will be the name that will be shown on the marketing campaign; as we are wanting to save the high street *as a whole*, not just individual businesses, this a team effort as all high street businesses are at stake.

In the marketing campaign, we need to include different ads that express different kinds of emotion, we also need to create ads that promotes a *cause* – which will be explaining how the high street can solve loneliness and how important the high street is to society. These ads will also remind people of an experience they get when shopping on the high street, that you don't get when shopping online. These ads will also include a powerful ad that will express what will happen to street performers, if the high street dies.

The ads will need to reflect both positive and negative emotions, the negative emotions will be stirred up in people, once they see how the ads reflect on who's lives will be impacted by the loss of the high street. The positive emotions will be stirred up in people, when people witness the ads express, what we get with the high street that we don't get online and what the high street can contribute to society, such as, shopping with your mates and having a laugh with each other while shopping.

Younger people are generally the geographic that shop more online than their elder counterparts, they are also more likely to tweet, or whatever they do. So when they see something emotional, they tweet about how it made them burst into tears or how amazing it made them felt when witnessing what they witnessed, they may even create memes because of it.

When people get emotional and become devoted to a cause as a result, it will create a *movement* of the masses, and when you have *the people* on your side, then that provides the leverage needed to pressure local councils and other entities, to solve the 'difficulties' that have contributed to the fall of the high street, such as parking prices and excessive rents.

These ads also need to be surprising. By which I mean, the major ads need to be displayed in places, where they do not normally advertise, such as, streaming services and the BBC alike. Why would they help in these matters? Well it goes back to the previous paragraph, the leverage that a mass movement gives you. We seen it with the recent GameStop movement against Wall Street, when people think collectively, anything can be achieved. Streaming services, may feel an obligation to participate in this movement, as they will be doing it for a good cause. The BBC, may be pressured to do it, as the BBC needs to give people a reason why the BBC still has a lot to contribute to society and why a T.V. license is still a valid form of payment. As more people are cancelling their license and avoiding T.V. altogether, they need to prevent a mass exodus of people leaving their service. If the BBC does a rare thing such as this, when they support a cause which will create a mass movement of people behind it, they will feel it's necessary to allow the advertisements of 'operation save the high street' as it's necessary in the national interest.

Why do they need to be surprising? Well, if you are watching on a channel, where they already use advertisements as a source of their income, then people generally mute the TV and go into the kitchen to make a cuppa, while the ads are playing. Therefore not really paying any attention. That's not to say we shouldn't advertise on these channels, because we should, for the few, that do indeed pay attention, but we should put more focus on the ones that will *hit better* with the viewers.

In order to make going to the high street 'cool'. We need to get U.K. celebrities to promote this movement, they will also feel an obligation to do it, as it's for a good cause and there's a mass movement of people behind it. Why U.K. celebrities? Well because, they were brought up in a time where the high street was the main place you go to in order to shop for everyday items, it's a better message for the people, when they are listening to celebrities who actually went shopping on high streets just like they did in the U.K. Some celebrities, may of even started out as street performers themselves, and will gladly share how that experience, helped them to become the person they are today.

We should also use more traditional forms of advertising, like leaflets; billboards and even placing posters about communication with other shoppers around retail stores.

When it comes to advertising on social media platforms, there should be dedicated pages that represent 'operation save the high street'. Which high street retailers already on Twitter should promote. These pages will be pushing cut down versions of the emotional ads shown on television and streaming services, they will be silent, with no words and short and sweet, but still powerful enough to cause a reaction from people.

WHAT SHOULD THE TELEVISED ADS ENTAIL? (4)

In this chapter we will be discussing the adverts in detail. Let's begin with the positive ads. The first one should show a group of girly friends who are strolling or dancing down the street, and then enter into a store, with some music playing and they are all dancing round in a circle, while holding hands, one breaks apart into the changing rooms, then the others also let go of each other's hands, they then get their phones out and as soon as their mate exits the changing room, they start taking videos, which they will then post onto their social stories, while, pulling positive faces expressing how *sexy* and how *beautiful* she looks, then the other friends will go in and out in a repeat process, with the focus being in the direction of the changing room, and it will be a 'quick, snap video transition' if you will, with each second there's a different girl, with a different style of clothing she is wearing, jumping out with a funny pose, in front of her friends who will be behind the camera. There will then be a transition into the end scene when they all line up and smile in front on the camera, then get blurred out, with the 'operation save the high street' logo and name and a strong voice taking over the scene saying 'save the high street, for an experience, you simply can't get online'.

The next positive ad, will start in a retail store, with people having a look and having a feel for the items. The shoppers will be spread out across different aisles or sections of the store. Then, suddenly, music starts playing; one person moves their head to their left in a dramatic way, then starts doing a robotic dance; then the one dancing suddenly does a 360 degree jump; the other shoppers from across the aisle, then looks at the one dancing. The person dancing then does a *'come over here'* hand motion and starts skipping round the aisles, with one shopper at a time following and mimicking the original dancer, then they all skip with the original dancer round the store for a bit, then they all face towards the camera, all dancing in the exact same way in sync with each other, then they end off the dance with arms over shoulders, they then get blurred out with the 'operation save the high street' logo and name and a strong voice taking over the scene saying 'saving the high street, by bringing people together'.

The next positive ad I will be describing, will be shorter than the previous ones. This ad, should involve a husband and wife, in the women's section of a store; particularly the bra section. The wife picks up a bra, then places it on herself, while placing the husbands hands on them. The both of them, then start giggling. The husband, then steps back, and gets the phone out and opens up the camera, then, takes a picture of his wife, posing with the bra, with her holding the bra on her chest, with her hands on them, then moving one leg to the side a bit and doing a cute smirk with her head down. The husband then shows off the photo to his wife and uploads it to Facebook, they then get back to shopping. The end scene comes in with the blurred out background and name and logo of 'operation save the high street'. A voice then comes in saying 'save the high street, for an experience, you simply can't get online'. But this time it should be a gentle females voice.

The next positive ad will also be a short one, it will focus on a conversation between shoppers. There will be a man having a look at clothes, then he goes up to a woman and asks 'hey, was wondering if you think this would look good on me?', she responds 'you know, I think it will, place it with this though'. She picks something up, then passes it to him, the video continues playing and they continue talking but they are muted, then the scene cuts off and the name and logo pops up, with a voice saying 'saving the high street can establish new connections, let's solve loneliness, let's save the high street together'.

The next ad, is neither positive or negative. It will show a husband and wife entering the store, the husband is bored to hell, shopping with his wife, as she never leaves and is there for hours, the husband then decides to leave the store and stand outside, waiting instead. Then, just stands round looking around him, as he sees closed down stores all over the street, he also sees a street performer across the street with a family watching him or her. The wife eventually finished shopping and shows her husband what she got, they then go on their way back home. The scene will then cut, with the logo and name of 'operation save the high street' popping up and a voice saying 'you may think you hate it, but you will end up missing it when it's gone; save the high street, as it's part of our culture'.

We will now move onto the ads that will fill people with *sadness* and *determination* to save the high street. The first one being solely focused on a street performer. The ad, should begin with a busy high street, on a sunny day, and a girl playing on a guitar and singing, she'll be sat down on a seat while doing so. Crowds of people will be chucking money into her guitar case, as they walk past, with some people around her, recording her with their phones. She'll continually sing the same song, while the scene gradually changes; the skies will begin to get darker and depressing, shops around her will gradually have their doors begin to shut, the people recording, will gradually just vanish in the scene, while people walking past, gradually blur out as they do so, until they pretty much look like a ghost walking by and then vanishing altogether. The money in the guitar case, gradually vanishes also, until eventually she finishes the song, she looks around, all shops have been abandoned, her guitar case is empty and the weather is dull. She begins to cry, as she does, the logo and name of 'operation save the high street' pops up with a voice saying 'a dead high street strips street performers of opportunity; let's save the high street together!'.

The next ad that will fill people with great *sadness* and *determination* will be reflective of the jobs that will be lost as a result of the death of the high street. It will show a young man, who is currently in school, walking down the high street and handing in a C.V. and asking the cashier that they are looking for a job. The cashier then takes the C.V. off the young man. The young man was then contacted by a manager via email, while he was sitting in McDonald's. He then was requested to come back the next day. On that day, he goes down the high street, he notices it isn't as busy as usual, he goes to the store to which he handed the C.V. To the cashier; he then sees that the doors have been shut and there's a notice on the door saying, that this store, will no longer be in operation and has laid-off all their staff. The young man then goes home and sees his parents, who are struggling with money and can barely feed themselves, he tells the parents that he was unable to get a job since half the high street has shut, *'there's no jobs I can get'* he says to his parents, they then start to cry. The scene then ends with them blurred out, with the logo and name of 'operation save the high street' and a voice says 'save the high street, save the jobs that many families depend on'.

The next ad will also be jobs focused, but this time it will be two managers, who operate separate stores and are across the street from each other. They live with each other and have children of their own and have their own staff. The scene will begin with each store manager leaving their stores at 17:00. They then go up to each other. One puts one arm over the other; they then walk home to see their kids. The scene then cuts to the kitchen of their home, they both serve dinner to their children and give each other a kiss before sitting down on the table. The scene shows a lot of laughing and smiling. The scene, then cuts into the morning, they both head to the office, only to hear the news that they will have to shut down their stores. The scene will show both manages with a 'split screen' showing them both on a phone and crying. They then go down to meet their staff, only to tell them, that they have to let them go. The staff get upset, some shouting at the managers and some just bursting into tears, the managers are now left with no income and become depressed. They go home to their kids, not knowing how long they can keep supporting the family or when they'll be able to get a job. The scene then cuts at the kitchen table, holding hands with their children and are tearful. The name and logo of 'operation save the high street' pops up, with a voice saying 'save the high street, as many families depend on it'.

The next ad will be focused on an elderly couple. They weren't brought up with technology, that does not mean they are not capable of using it, but it is a lot harder for elderly couples to use technology, as it's something *new* for them. The elderly couple in this ad will only have a television. They do not own a computer or have access to the internet.

The scene will begin, with a 70 year old lady and her 76 year old husband. They are at home. The husband is planning on going to the shops to buy some socks, as his current ones all have holes in them. The wife says to the husband *'would you mind if I come with? I could use a new dress for next weeks dinner with our family'*. The husband says *'oh alright then'*. They then go and watch some television, they go onto the news and hear that the high street shops in their local area has shut down. They are startled! They ask each other *'well what are we going to do now?!?'*. They get upset while sitting on the couch. They then, decide to ring their family, if they could buy some clothes for them. But the family lives nearly two hours away, so they'll have to wait until dinner in a few weeks time. The scene then cuts to the moment they are all having dinner. The family, gives the elderly couple new pairs of socks and a dress. But the dress was only wanted for the dinner, so, she ended up wearing one of her old dresses, which, you could see that she needed a new one. They then say *'thank you'*. The family then asks politely, *'why don't you get yourselves a computer and you can shop online?'*. They respond with *'we have experimented on another's computer before, but it's to difficult, with the size tables and measurements and the experience is not for us, we don't like to spend money on an irritating experience, we get anxiety'*. The scene then cuts to the logo and name of 'operation save the high street' and a voice saying 'save the high street, because not everyone can shop online'.

WHAT SHOULD THE LEAFLETS ENTAIL? (5)

In this chapter, we'll be discussing what the leaflets should include. We should have multiple leaflets, that reflect the importance of the high street. One of them focused on how the high street can solve loneliness. The other, expressing an experience. The other focusing on how the high street can save street performers and the other, showing the impact that it will have in working families, if the high street dies.

On the front of every leaflet, it should have 'Save The High Street' to catch people's eye. People tend to ignore leaflets, (at least in my experience) if you are advertising a product. But if you are advertising a *cause*, then I tend to think people take more of an interest.

Let's begin with the first leaflet, as well as 'Save The High Street' on the front page, this one should include 'it's the key to solving loneliness'. With dimmed images of people talking in the aisles of the stores in the background. Inside the leaflet should, simply include examples of how to start conversations with fellow shoppers. It should also include an image of someone holding clothes and someone next to them engaging into a conversation, with information on why it's important to save the high street to help people who are feeling lonely.

The next leaflet should talk about an experience, that you get when shopping on the high street that you don't get online. It should include an image on the front page, that shows someone touching and feeling the items; the changing rooms and the in person customer service. The front page, along side the *eye catching* 'save the high street' text. Should say in small text 'for an experience you can't get anywhere else'. Inside the leaflet, should include more information and include more detail, about the experience of being able to shop on the high street and to feel and try the items yourself, rather than relying on images and size tables online.

The next leaflet, should focus on the street performers and how they benefit from the high street. The front page should include a photograph of a street performer on the high street, with a guitar and microphone; singing away. Next to the title 'Save The High Street' should include a subtitle saying 'a dead high street strips opportunity from street performers'. Inside the leaflet, should explain how street performers need the high street, as it's the best opportunity for them to get out there and reach people.

The final leaflet, should focus on the jobs that will be lost as result of a dying high street and how so many working and middle class families depend on them. The front page of the leaflet, should of course include the title 'save the high street' with a subtitle saying 'as so many families depend on it'. Inside the leaflet, should include information on how families will be impacted by the loss of jobs, how it may impact the reader personally, if they ever end up in the same situation as most struggling families.

All leaflets, should have images behind the text describing the situations to give it a more emotional appeal to the reader. This should be the case for both the inside and outside of the leaflets.

Ian Mason

WHAT SHOULD THE BILLBOARD ADS ENTAIL? (6)

In this chapter, we'll be discussing what the billboards should express for the campaign to save the high street and where they should be located.

Let's begin with the first billboard. The first billboard should show celebrities, who were once street performers and are now where they are today. They should include a large image of them, with a quote beside the image, which, explains how the high street helped them get where they are at today. These celebrities, shouldn't only include *big shot* celebrities, but also up and coming ones, such as, YouTube music stars, or songwriters and singers which have songs which have reached the top charts on music streaming services.

The billboards for the above, should be located on the motorway, and in city centres.

The next billboard, will also be about street performers, but not past ones or celebrities. This one should just be focused on your everyday street performer, who make themselves a bit of income while performing on the high street. There will be a large image, of them performing, with a message beside the image saying that they rely on the high street, it provides them with opportunity. This billboard, should be shown on the remaining High Streets that are doing well and should be placed near coffee shops.

The next billboard, will be about a value that the high street stands for, which is of course, solving loneliness. It should show an image of two people shaking hands and smiling at each other. There should be text next to the image saying 'communicate with fellow shoppers, the high street can solve loneliness'. This billboard, should be located on bus stop display panels and on high traffic streets.

The next billboard, will be about the experience you get when shopping on the high street, that you don't get online. It should show an image of someone touching an item with text beside the image saying 'you can't do this with online shopping'. This billboard should be located in the same areas as the previous one.

POSTERS IN STORES (7)

Now let's move onto the posters in retail stores. Posters should just give the message to shoppers about having a conversation with other shoppers. These posters should include illustrations of people that are talking, they should simply be black and white. A white background and bold black text. The posters should also be simple, no added text or anything. Just a simple; bold statement.

Posters should be placed all around the stores. The entrance; the aisles and the wall just before getting on an escalator.

These posters are just to encourage people to communicate with other shoppers to solve loneliness, for those who have not seen the ads.

SOCIAL MEDIA PAGES (8)

In this chapter, we'll expand on what 'operation save the high street' social media pages should do, beyond promoting the advertisements. The social media pages, should engage with people who are commenting on the ads with sites like Twitter. When someone tweets about how emotional the ad is, the 'operation save the high street' page should engage with the tweeter, with a reply that nudges the tweeter, to give a follow and partake in the mission to save the high street. The Twitter (or sites like it) page, should encourage people, during the marketing campaign, to share their stories about how they made a new friend with the whole "communicate with fellow shoppers" *thing* and to share a photo of them meeting in a shop. The Twitter page should also tag celebrities, who have been asked to make videos on why we should all partake in saving the high street. The page, should both reply and quote the tweet the celebrity made, to encourage people further, into saving the high street. The Twitter page should also partake in a little humour with people who follow the page.

The Instagram page, should focus on promoting slide show images. Kind of like, when someone uploads an image of their car, they only take one picture of the front end, for the first image. They then take a picture of the middle, for people to slide onto the second image. Then for the final image they upload the back of the car. As a result, you have the whole car, just split into multiple images that people need to swipe, in order to see the whole car. We should apply this method for our save the high street Instagram page. The images should show the same two people, but the first image, should show them having a conversation with each other, with text on the image saying 'saving the high street can solve loneliness, communicate with your fellow shoppers, even if you don't know them. So many people could use a good talk with someone, it can make their day.' The second image, should show the two people touching and trying on the item, with text on the image saying 'you can't do this online, save the high street'. The third image, should show the two people, but with friends around them and having a laugh with certain items of clothing. The text on the third image should say 'save the high street, for an experience you cannot get online!'.

That was the final image for one post. But another post should show a street performer. Using the same method. The first image should show the street performer, on a sunny day, with open shops and a busy street with people watching them. The following images of the post, should gradually get more depressing, as the more you swipe, the more shops you see shut and the less people you see on the street watching the performance. The skies should also get darker throughout each image to make it more *dramatic*. The caption for the post should be 'save the high street, as a dead high street strips opportunity from street performers'.

The final post, should be representative of the job situation if the high street dies and what families will be impacted. Using the same method. The first image should be a family at the table, with a husband; wife and kids. The first image, should be full of happiness at the table with food on the plates, but the more images you slide across, the more the mood changes in their faces. Food gradually disappears, until, it gets to the point when they are all holding hands and crying with no food on the table. The caption should be 'save the high street, as many families depend on it'.

Now the Instagram page has three posts which puts it out there on why the high street needs saving. The page should then post and focus on stories, and encourage its followers to tag them in a story, in hopes of getting a shout out. The story of the follower could be a photo of people meeting for the first time in a high street shop or it could show how important the high street is to their lives. The Instagram page should then share that story, with a tag of the followers personal Instagram page. This helps people engage more, and to share the page to their friends and family who are also on Instagram.

The Instagram page should also post glimpses of the televised ads onto stories.

The Snapchat page for 'operation save the high street' should give in person snap examples to its followers. There should be a representative, going to random shops on the high street and communicating with fellow shoppers, to help encourage others to do the same. The snap should have a caption saying 'just gonna go to the shops and talk to folk'. It can be the same to show other practices to save the high street, there should be an individual giving a practical example of the ways we can save the high street and uploading it on snap.

The Facebook page for 'operation save the high street' should simply share everything from all social media pages in one bubble and promote the pages on Facebook, there should be a community page, where people can discuss topics and contribute their own opinions on saving the high street also.

All social media pages may have their own uses, but they should also have links to each other, so people know where to go to get a different perspective. Where they can follow on all platforms, not just a singular one.

Celebrities may have only been mentioned in the Twitter section, but celebrities should also be encouraged to post on other social media platforms also.

SOCIAL MEDIA PAGES AND MEMES (9)

In this chapter, we will discuss more creative ways for the social media pages to communicate with the public. With memes specifically.

All social media pages, apart from Snapchat should be sharing memes to the followers. What type of memes?

Well they need engagement, so, we need to combine humorous text with high street related images. An example would be the jealous couple one. This one contains both a boyfriend and girlfriend, while, the boyfriend takes a glance behind him to look in a lustful way at another girl walking past. The faces of these people should be replaced with the related topic. The girlfriend should represent online shopping, the boyfriend should represent the consumer and the girl walking past should represent the high street. The text should say 'looking to take the wife shopping'. This is just one idea, but whoever this reaches, should obviously come up with their own ideas for the memes also. Memes are one of the main ways people communicate with each other in today's world, simple text but meaningful images that create engagement and are understood better than traditional messages. Memes should be posted on Twitter and Facebooks feed all the time. The memes should also be posted on Instagram stories.

INTERVIEWS (10)

In this chapter, we'll be discussing the interviews that are bound to happen, if the movement gains momentum. The key people behind the movement, should be going on television or radio or any other type of interviews to describe what the whole movement is about in depth. The ones who will be doing interviews, should be passionate and enthusiastic about the movement, in order to sell it to people. There needs to be an *energy* behind what they are saying.

The people who will be discussing it, should not only do traditional interviews, but even go onto comedy shows and talk with *talk show* hosts.

When being on an interview, they should discuss all the values the high street stands for, such as solving loneliness. They should also remind people of the experience which you get shopping on the street, that you certainly do not get online and what steps are being taken in order to save the high street.

EVIDENCE THAT THIS WILL WORK (11)

In this chapter, we'll take a look of past and present examples of how this method of marketing has worked and how simply getting people to view something on a screen can make them feel like they are connected to what's going on emotionally.

Let's start off with Hollywood blockbusters, Hollywood creates movies and develops characters that relate to people in some way. Titanic was a love story, it connected with people who have always dreamed about finding true love and even post death, the love never faded, it was always there and never forgotten about. It ended with a very sad scene, they were with each other up until the end. It made the audience burst into tears and is still wildly talked about to this day.

An example of a television show, is 'FRIENDS' which was an American show, which included a group of friends who hung out all the time, were always there for each other. The show was a comedy, but one of the reasons it was so popular, was because the people watching, felt like they were that group of friends themselves. It called out to the viewers and really connected the characters and the audience, it's still talked about today despite the fact it came out decades ago. They felt on an emotional level, that they were friends with the characters and it was a reflection of the viewers personal friendships.

Now let's move onto examples of companies that have used this marketing tactic, we are going to expand on the example which was given in the introduction of the book. Apple and an extra one, Nike.

Let's start off with Nike. A company that rarely; if ever advertises the product. A company that creates ads that really connects with people emotionally. A company that advertises the values of which they stand for. Nike creates the most incredible ads and they are one of the best brands in the whole world. They honour great athletes and they advertise the sport. Let me give an example of their advertising. (Type this link between the '<>')

< https://youtu.be/WA4dDs0T7sM >. This ad represents unity and equality and determination. The products are not mentioned once, they are only seen by the athletes wearing them. But, this single ad has got an extraordinarily high engagement with high ratings, because people feel more connected to the values, more than the product, which then makes them feel a certain respect to Nike and makes them want to go out and buy their products.

Now let's move onto Apple. Specifically back in the 90s when they were 90 days from bankruptcy. They created a magnificent marketing campaign, that also represented values. It was named 'Think Different'. This campaign honoured those who have changed the world and it gave a message to the public, that Apple was expressing what they believed in. That people with passion, can change the world for the better. Here's a link to their ad: < https://youtu.be/5sMBhDv4sik >. Not once is a product mentioned in this ad. What this ad did, was bring Apple back onto the map, it sent a message to people that *'we are different'* and *we believe you can be different too'*. It gave people a new found respect for the company, it gave people hope that they can (with their 'tools') also make a difference in life. The ad showed people; both past and present, who changed the world, both in some big and some small way. They not only made a televised ad, but they placed billboards all over the place, that showed a face of someone who have changed the world, some who are wildly known, but also those who were lesser known to the world or forgotten about. This ad, made people think that this company was different, it connected people to the company and it said to people *'you know, I feel like moving to Apple products over my current ones'*. It also gave a message to people, that they were more than just a number, the company that they were buying from actually believed in them.

Now let's move onto news outlets, yes, they don't advertise products whatsoever, but that's not the point of this one. News outlets always exaggerate and love to post negative stories. Why? Because people don't click on positive news, more people click on the negative news because they want to know what's going on and how it can impact them. But even if it doesn't impact them, if it's negative they'll click on it, because they like to talk about sad things too. What do the news outlets do with negative posts? Well they like to exaggerate, they like to be overly dramatic about it. The more depressing and sad they make an article, the better for them. The more a story can stir up controversy, the better. The more a story can stir up anger the better. It's what news outlets do. They tell the truth, but they manipulate it, in a way that will get the most clicks. They play with emotions all the time. It attracts people to listen to what they are saying and gets people to take action.

WHY WE SHOULD NOT TACKLE ONLINE SHOPPING WITH EXTRA TAXES (12)

In this chapter, we'll discuss why we shouldn't go on the attack against online shopping with taxes and instead just leave online shopping as it is.

This whole book is based on the principle that there's room for both online and high street shopping, without attacking the other with taxes and frowning upon those who do. This book is to simply separate both ways of shopping altogether. Yes, online shopping has been a major factor in the diminishing high street. But, online shopping has provided so much opportunity for many people out there. Many people have income that is reliant on online commerce. They may sell on Amazon or have a successful shop on Etsy, they may be based on a royalty based website like Spreadshirt and others. If you increase taxes for online retail, then royalties may be cut, income for those families who rely on e-commerce may be cut. We shouldn't increase taxes anywhere, taxes lead to nothing but trouble. We should just encourage people to go and shop around and if they can't find what they are looking for, then they can go online. Online for unique items that you can't find locally and shop locally for items you can get in your local high street and shop on the high street for the values which were mentioned in the advertisements.

Online shopping, also makes it easier to shop for those who struggle with crowds and have disabilities. So by increasing taxes on e-commerce. Then you are merely passing on extra costs to the consumers that rely on e-commerce for items, that aren't available locally and for them personally, as they find it hard to go out and shop.

HOW RETAIL AND LOCAL COUNCILS CAN WORK TOGETHER WITH INNOVATIVE IDEAS FOR PARKING (13)

In this chapter, we'll discuss innovative ways on areas where retail and councils can work together on in terms of parking.

Many local councils are struggling with funds, whether this is due to overspending or being underfunded is up for debate. However, when it comes to parking, there are ways to help get consumers to still pay, but at the same time provide an incentive for consumers to consider still going out.

Let's consider this idea, this may require new parking meter machines, however it starts like this. You pay for your parking for so many hours, but retail stores offer a deal *'buy 2 or more items to get a parking discount receipt'*. With this receipt, once you return from shopping, you can then scan this receipt in the machine, which will either give you a refund of 50% off your ticket price, or refund you altogether, depending on how much the retailer is willing to offer. Obviously there should be a limit to how many hours this will work still, as you don't want people hogging the parking space all day or to rip retailers off, but if done correctly; then this could help encourage consumers to shop on the high street and spend more money on goods and help local councils maintain levels of income needed for public services.

Another idea, is for a monthly fee for those who go shopping often, instead of paying parking every time they go out to shop. They pay a monthly subscription instead. There should be multiple options and the cost should depend on vehicle size and your personal income also. This subscription service should be set up by companies instead of the council. You can decide to choose Next or New Look for your subscription model for instance. This creates competition, and with this subscription, they may get discounts on items like dresses or hats etc. 20% of the income of this subscription should go to local councils, as long as they pledge to use at least half of this money to open up more parking facilities for shoppers, with the rest being spent on vital public services like public transport, which they should provide free bus travel if they get this extra money, which should also in turn help more people to shop.

LEVERAGE OF THE PEOPLE TO MAKE DEALS (14)

In chapter 2, leverage was mentioned. In this chapter, we'll expand on that topic. The people provide you with leverage. With this movement, you can use the people to the high streets advantage. This is to solve the high streets more technical problems, such as business rates reform. Lower taxes altogether etc. You can only pressure politicians to push forward with this, when you have the country unified in one collective view, if the majority are in favour of saving the high street (which, assuming they've took notice of the ads etc. Then yes they would be). Then politicians will have no choice but to push forward with the changes needed to be done and for the private and public sector to work together, in saving the high street as quickly as possible. With the leverage of a mass movement, the deals that can be made will certainly be a lot easier.

It's not only politicians that you can pressure, but when you have the country behind you. You can pressure any entity to make any deal that will be beneficial for the high street.

SAVED THE HIGH STREET (15)

Following these steps, combined with the innovative ideas of others can save the high street. The high street still has a chance to make a comeback, so, hopefully this book reached the right people because we need to save the high street sooner, rather than later. Let's save the high street together! Let's save our communities and change the culture of this country which promotes communication and establishes new connections, which will unify the country.

INDEX

AUTHOR CONTACTS

Twitter: @REALIANMASON or @IBMClothing – message on their for anything you may need off the author.